Shopping

By Sally Hewitt
Photographs by Chris Fairclough

FRANKLIN WATTS
LONDON • SYDNEY

This edition 2004

Franklin Watts
96 Leonard Street
London EC2A 4XD

Franklin Watts Australia
45-51 Huntley Street
Alexandria
NSW 2015

Editor: Samantha Armstrong
Consultant: Steven Watts, School of Education, University of Sunderland
Designer: Louise Snowdon
Photographs: Chris Fairclough

A CIP catalogue record for this book is
available from the British Library
Dewey Decimal Classification Number: 381

ISBN 0 7496 5202 0

Printed in Malaysia

Contents

The farm shop

The flowers, fruit and vegetables on sale at this shop are all fresh from the farm.

• Did the goods come a long way from the farm to the shop?
• Can you buy these goods in a supermarket?
• Do you think they are cheaper or more expensive here than at a supermarket?

The chalkboard tells customers about today's special offers.

• Is a chalkboard a good way to give information?
• How do other shops display special offers?

The strawberries look juicy and bright red. The carrots look orange and crunchy.

• Would you like to buy your fruit and vegetables at the farm shop? Why?
• How would you carry the things you wanted to buy?

The market

This open-air market happens on Wednesdays and Saturdays. Market stalls can be set up and taken down quickly and easily.

- What do you think this street looks and sounds like when it isn't market day?
- What will the customers in the market need on a rainy day?

Money in a shop is usually kept in a till. The market stall holder zips money into her apron pocket.

- Why do you think this is a good place to keep money?

A man pulls a cart full of goods to sell in the market.

• Why is a cart used instead of a truck?

At the end of the day, the stalls are packed away.

• What does a shop look like just before it closes? How is it different from the market stall?

The local shop

A local shop is packed with the goods that people living nearby need to buy from day to day.

- What would you find for sale in a local shop like this?
- How can you tell if the customers in the picture live locally or if they are passing by?

This shop is a post office as well.

- Why do you think this is useful?
- What else can you buy or have done for you at this shop?

The next shop is a long way away!

- What does this sign tell you to do? Why?
- What might you want to buy in the shop if you were going to Kinlochleven?

Specialist shops

The butcher's, the baker's, the carpet mart and the fruit shop are all specialist shops. They sell particular types of goods.

- What do the shops in the photographs on these pages sell?
- What other specialist shops might you find?
- How would the baker's shop smell? Would the fruit shop smell the same?

Specialist shop owners get to know the customers who come every week.

- What kind of meat does the butcher's shop in this picture sell? Do you know who might buy it?
- How is a butcher's shop different from a supermarket meat counter?

- What do you think the carpet mart looks like inside?

The high street

Shops and businesses line both sides of this busy high street. You can go to the high street to shop, to visit the bank or to have your eyes tested.

- What else can you do on this high street?
- Can you spot different ways of getting here?
- Where would you cross the road to shop on the other side?

14

A department store

A department store is a shop which sells lots of different products. It usually has more than one floor. There are several departments on each floor.

- Can you see the women's clothes department through the windows on the first floor?
- What department would you choose to put on the ground floor? Why?

- In which departments would you find the goods shown in the three photographs on this page?
- In a department store how would you find out where to get something special like football boots or a pair of shoes?

A shopping centre

In a shopping centre there are all kinds of different shops and places to eat. You could stay there all day.

- Would you like to shop at this shopping centre?
- Why?

People can see all around them as they go up and down in the lifts or on the escalators.

• Can you see the glass lifts in the main picture?
• Why do you think it is a good idea for customers to be able to see the shopping centre from the lifts and escalators?

Sun shines through the roof, and plants grow in tubs and hanging baskets.

• What do you think the shopping centre looks and feels like on a dark, cold day?

19

A supermarket

When you go shopping in a big supermarket, fresh food in chiller cabinets, frozen food in big freezers, food in packets, jars and tins are just some of the things to choose from.

- What else can you buy in a supermarket?
- Think about the farm shop. Where do you think the products in the supermarket come from?

At the checkout, each piece of shopping is put in front of a scanner.

The scanner reads a barcode on the shopping and the price is printed on the receipt.

• Which items in the supermarket may not have a barcode on them?

A trolley full of shopping fills a lot of bags.

• What different ways could the customer get all this shopping home?

21

Outside a supermarket

There is plenty of space outside this supermarket for a big car park.

- What kind of car park might there be for a supermarket in a busy town centre?
- Apart from by car, how could customers get to the supermarket?

This picture shows shopping being loaded into a car.

- How far does this customer have to carry all this heavy shopping?

Newspapers, bottles and cans are collected for recycling.

- What else could you do or buy on a trip to this supermarket?

Coffee Shop
Cash Dispensers
Photo Processing
Toilets
Recycling Centre

Out-of-town shopping

This retail park is out of town. The shops have space for selling big things like furniture or computers. Customers can park near the shop they want to visit.

- How are the shops in a retail park different from the shops in a town centre?
- How are they the same?

24

Two people work out how to fit their shopping into the back of the car.

- How else could they get the shopping home?

There are three different shapes of trolley.

- Why aren't all the trolleys the same shape?

A special bus service runs between the retail park and the town centre.

- Why could using the bus be a good idea?

On-line shopping

Shopping can be done without leaving home.
You can choose what you want from a catalogue
and order it by post or over the telephone; or turn
on the computer and shop on-line on the Internet.

• When is it helpful to shop without leaving home?

When you shop on the Internet
information about items for
sale is shown on the
computer screen.

• What would you need
to know?
• How is this different
from choosing what you
want to buy in a shop?

To make the payment,
you type in your
credit card number.

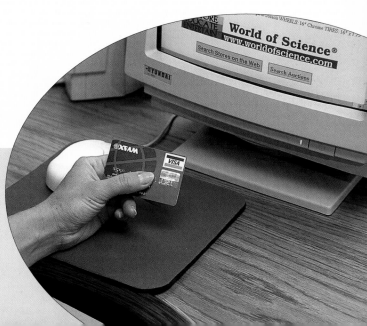

• What other information
would you have to type in
to make sure your shopping
arrived at your home?

Key words

Barcode   thick and thin lines printed onto goods for sale. A computer reads the code and prints the price and information about the goods onto a receipt.

Business   another word for a place of work. Shops and offices are different kinds of businesses.

Credit card   a plastic card that can be used to buy goods instead of cash. The card owner pays when they get a bill.

Customer   someone who goes into a shop, or any other business, to buy something.

Department   an area in a store where particular kinds of goods are sold.

Goods   products or items to buy.

Information   everything you can know about anything. Information about something for sale could be how much it costs and how much it weighs.

Local   everything in your neighbourhood that is within walking distance.

On-line shopping   shopping done through a computer linked to the Internet.

Receipt   a printed ticket that proves you have paid for your shopping.

Recycling   reusing things like old newspapers, bottles and cans. They are collected and taken away to be made into something new.

Retail park   a park built only for shops and shoppers.

Scanner   a scanner at the supermarket checkout reads the barcode on what you are buying.

Specialist shops   shops that sell only one type of good.

Think about shopping

1. Find out which shop is nearest to where you live.
   - How long does it take you to get there?
   - What does it sell?

2. Make a shopping list for a party. You will need invitations, food, prizes and decorations.
   - What shops would you have to go to for everything on the list?

3. When you go shopping, make a note of the specialist shops you see.
   - Which shop sells the most unusual specialist goods?

4. Imagine you own a shop. Draw a plan of your shop.
   - Is it a big department store, a small specialist shop or even a market stall?
   - How will you decide where to put your goods?
   - What can you do to get people to come inside the shop to buy your goods?

5. When you go shopping in a supermarket, make a note of all the different jobs you see everyone doing.

Index